STRUCK BY LIGHTNING AND ...

WOKE UP GIGGLING!

PAMELA STORRS

Struck by lightning and ...

Woke Up Giggling!

By Pamela Storrs

Copyright 2015 Pamela Storrs

Published by Winston Words Publishing

www.WinstonWordsPublishing.com

ISBN: 978-0-9828079-2-7

For my extraordinary husband and your gentle soul on this journey. Our souls are one.

Acknowledgments

So many people to be grateful for on this journey! Thanks to my husband Jim, for your patience and assistance as the V.P. of E.I. (Everything Important!). Fran, my goodness! Even though you don't want credit for editing, without your honesty and guidance, this book would not be half of what it is (literally)! Thank you, and your fabulous Ray and Shadow, for our rich conversations and friendship.

Such gratitude for the lifetime friends around the globe; you know who you are! Thanks to my birth and soul families, for being on this journey; I hope I have inspired you as much as you have inspired me. And to our group of fabulous Florida friends, who keep us sane ... (ha!). And my soul sisters here, you have enriched my life immeasurably.

I haven't named names in this writing ... and have omitted so much of our interactions in this life! Only because there just isn't enough room for it all in one book! Perhaps the next books will be fiction based on fact so that I might take a bit more liberty in the writings, and include more of you! I'm thankful for you.

Table of Contents

Souls have communicated with me

Souls have communicated with me ever since I was a small girl. Deceased souls wanting to talk with their loved ones still living, and souls hanging around to smile and give guidance. It wasn't until I was 8 or 9 years old that I realized who they were and could distinguish between the living and those crossed over. Being in this flow of energy, in awareness of my Soul as within the physical body, and not separate from it; that which we have named intuition (the knowledge that is always present) was also always the flow I lived in. I had knowledge of people's thoughts and emotions, their illnesses, griefs, judgments, limited vision of life, life journeys, and most predominately the potential of their soul in this body in this lifetime. Since no one had told me otherwise, of course I thought that everyone knew everything about everyone else! No one ever told me what to do with this information, and it was and is such a loving flow ... so I observed, was incredibly shy (what's there to talk about?), and learned about human nature.

Elementary school was interesting; I loved to learn, though I was at my own pace, and soaking up so much more, apparently, than others. In second grade or so, each of us sitting properly at our little desks, the teacher was explaining something by drawing on the chalkboard and thinking "Where is that eraser?" "What will I do when I need it to go on to the next lesson?" Only shyness kept me in my seat and not responding to her unspoken questions ... and I watched the other kids responding to her spoken and written words. So I learned what to respond to out loud, but not how to shut off the incoming thoughts (nor did it occur to me then to do so).

Always, the deceased souls emanated Joy and a deep peace, and that feeling was ever present in my life. The distress came from the human emotions of others; the unresolved stuff emanating from everyone living. Of course a young girl would pay attention to those who are harmless (the deceased), and shy away from those who experience such emotional pain and judgmental thoughts in their ignorance of the whole story of others around them (the living).

It was only on occasion that souls trapped "in between" appeared to me. It was then I began to develop filters and enhanced protection for myself to better live my life in this way, in the flow, as my journey was not to focus on those "stuck". I can help them move on, though it's for me to pass on messages from those who have crossed over. It's a joy to communicate with those who exist as souls in Life beyond this; whether you call it heaven, Nirvana, or something else ... it's the same place.

It is a place void of the human emotions, though there is an astounding awareness from those souls of the events and emotions we experience here on Earth. Life after Life is ultimate awareness and wisdom, with joy beyond imagination.

On My Journey!

Alaska ... the early years

When I was a little girl growing up I apparently didn't like to wear shoes. So off they came as soon as they were put on my feet. A bit of an issue at 50 below, especially in Fairbanks, Alaska! Half a century later, I live in the subtropics, so most all my shoes now are sandals ... casual ones, pretty ones, funny pairs too. And I still do prefer to be barefoot, and on the sand or in the water! Since I had lived on islands for a while, by the time I moved to Colorado in the late 90s I had a collection of open toed shoes for summertime.

But I got ahead of myself, so let me back up ... I was born in the middle of the winter, the darkest and coldest time of year. What in the world was I thinking!? I'm so grateful, though, for all of the experiences and friendships in that special place.

I never did see an igloo, as we lived in a regular house, and went through a fabulous school system. The Earth is quite rich in the interior of Alaska, with a semi-arid climate, and was largely unspoiled, so growing your own vegetables and herbs (which is now "organic" or "sustainable") was commonplace. And with entire days of sunlight in the summer (essentially no darkness falls), there were contests at the state fair for the largest ... pumpkins, zucchini, broccoli, etc. We're talking 30 to 50 pounders! Digging in the dirt to unearth a carrot there is unparalleled! So sweet. Come September, the moose come to eat the remainders ... they're so large, they just step on over the fence.

I was about 9 or so when some moose found their way into the family garden; cauliflower seemed to be their favorite of the day. We were all watching from the window when I declared that I wanted to go out and see these creatures up close. As I snuck quietly around the house, I was still fifty feet or so away when they came into view ... what enormous powerful animals (1000 pounds at least)! One snorted, and the smell was louder than the sound, an overpowering stench from this primal beast! Needless to say, it was close enough for a little girl, so in I scurried, flushed and excited and just a little in awe. Watching these creatures dine out from inside was entertaining enough.

Indeed there were adventures for us kids that we took in as though it was a wonderful world, not always realizing how unique and special Alaska is. Hiking once as a small girl, with my Dad and brothers, had us smallest ones crawling through a beaver hut rather than over it, as the water level had dropped so much ... who else have been in the house where beavers live? No beavers were home at the time (and we hope we didn't leave behind any energy that would scare them away), and one could notice how these simple creatures rested, slept and built ... their homes, their environment ... protecting the water levels with their huts.

Fragrant low bush cranberries, pungent high bush cranberries, and the best blueberries (when they weren't stripped from their bushes by the bears) kept us going for hours. What treats these berries were ... growing beautifully wild, prolifically.   Us, the wilderness, the creatures ... we were taught to walk softly and purposefully, in awareness and tuned in to nature. Listening to the silence, asking what each sound is; which bird? A squirrel? Is that a bear snorting? Make noise to scare that one off! (They are more scared of us strange wildlife invading their environment). This pace keeps one grounded, peaceful and in the flow of Earth, its natural state and all the Universe.

On My Journey!

What I knew

Barely taller than the stove, I was about 6 years old when I stood by it watching Mom cook one beautiful summer day. She asked me why I wasn't outside playing with the other kids? I told her that the phone was going to ring in a minute, and was amazed that she was asking about that. She asked who was going to call, and I told her the name of the boy from kindergarten ... he was about to call and invite me to his birthday party. I knew this, and was amazed that she was asking what, of course, she knew too! Mom's verbal response was that if he had already asked me, it was okay. I could go, she'd just need to talk to his Mom. What was she thinking! School was a long time ago; when could he have asked? At the same time, I saw her thoughts and feelings ... first the practical, and then ... oh no! Her daughter has "the sight" ... how do you deal with that? For me, it was a new concept of time, and the understanding of linear time that some humans make so that life is in some sort of order. How could I *not* know this was going to happen!? That was my question. She had three other children to raise, so how could she pay attention to her own intuition and raise them in this world, and then this one!!

Needless to say, the phone rang; and I went to my first party.

In retrospect, if she could only have seen the "time saving benefits" of being in the flow ... the simple answer of "Yes, you can go. Be sure to put his Mom on the phone!" ... this would have felt ordinary to me. Our society for the most part, is not connected and centered well enough for this to occur often. Sometimes, you'll find yourself finishing another's sentence or speaking the same thing at the same time; this is being in the flow. And it does not get boring, if you're asking! It's just a matter of this time/space continuum, and how we relate to each other, how much we want to pay attention, and how much we want to find our calm, joyful center.

Thus the beginning of keeping to myself what I "knew" until I saw or heard what others acknowledged that they knew intuitively. Over time people asked me for my "opinion" quite often ... turns out they didn't want my intellectual opinion, but truly my intuition about them. Decades later (I had to live my own journey, you know!), it is how I live and what I do ... share the intuition with whomever is asking for it. You name it ... how I share my gifts or curses, that is ... as an Intuitive, a Listener, a Seer, a Psychic, a Medium, an Empath, a Psychometrist, a Healer, a Medical Intuitive, a Spiritual Advisor, a Fairy GodMentor, a Power House, etc. ... it's all within the same flow. We are all a soul within a body, so yes, we all came with "abilities"; it's a matter of what we pay attention to that we develop. A few, like myself, are what I call "full blown" (or every which way but loose!), whole people, and there is nothing we are not in flow with, except by choice.

A runner may always be training, and mostly focused on the physical; eating and exercising to enhance endurance and strength; a banker might always be looking at the numbers, thinking and rethinking. It's what we focus on and think about that makes us who we are. We are physical, mental, emotional and spiritual beings; a balance makes us whole.

During recess in early elementary school, amongst all the wonderful kids, there were three of us little girls who gravitated to each other and become special friends. Sometimes, we would just sit quietly under a big tree during the warmer weather and watch the other kids at play, no need to speak, just being delighted together. After a time, an adult asked me "Don't you like one of those two girls better than the other?" Well, no! But I looked (as I do; into the ethers) and saw and felt each as they are; both of the same gentle energy as I, one being mostly pinks, quiet oranges and yellows, the other such pleasant blues, bright gold and lavenders. Then I saw through the adult's eyes ... their skin color!

Wow, I had never focused on skin colors, as what I now know as auras have always been so present, visible and palpable to me. And I saw the ignorant judgment (of auras and energy) of generations past in this adult; she was, however, not so stuck on that judgment that was passed to her that she wasn't interested in what I might be seeing. I saw this, and said: "I like them just the same! Are you really asking me to choose one over the other? Why? Aren't we supposed to have more than one friend at a time? I can't choose." That would be like limiting love, dividing it, and shunning someone because their pancreas is green (that's my thought now), and I didn't know how. She shifted. The three of us girls remained friends, and the parents became friends. I grew up with people of all nationalities, the various Alaskan Natives, Caucasians, Asians, African Americans, people of planet Earth. I saw their souls, their similarities and their differences, in their auras. Such beautiful human beings. Because of our own doing, we girls just continued to flow. From the lives of babes!

On My Journey With Others!

Up in the air ... in a plane

At 17, I went up (in the air) in a Supercub. As in *flew* ... in the quintessential north country bush airplane; a tail dragger with tandem seats (one behind the other). It was the most thrilling, passion evoking and natural experience of my life so far, and I understood that day what an intention is. I would learn to fly as certainly as I breathed, it simply was to be, and I knew it. Not because of determination, but because of pure joy, desire and the understanding that anything is possible if you imagine it so. And flying in Alaska is commonplace, so it wasn't at all a far fetched idea. And this experience of flight was pure bliss.

My airplane, a red and white Citabria 7GCBC, was also a tail dragger with tandem seats, and it sported tundra tires (oversized, with flexible gear), which I would replace with skis in the winter ... so many places to land when the Earth is snow covered and frozen! And summertime flying out to a river to fish or hike; not another soul around for at least a hundred miles (well, no human souls, anyway). Fly-ins with friends to remote lakes to camp, taking people up to see the country and the animals from the air or just to go UP! was my joy. As with many "bush" planes in Alaska, mine was capable of short take offs and landings ... and my oh my, the places she and I went and were able to land and take off from! Sand bars, the sides of mountains, tiny little "airstrips" put in by friends ... you become one with your plane if you choose to.

Flying, up and around, to return to Earth where I left it, sheds all the stuff of daily life. It gives a free perspective to all that is, and the mental strain disappears. Perhaps that's why I learned to go upside down in my plane; loops and such ... aerobatics. Freedom and ease. Perspective. The clearing of all things.

One day, Betty Fahrenkamp, former State Senator, and former elementary school teacher of mine, convinced me and some other gal fliers to start a Fairbanks chapter of the 99s ... the international organization first begun by Amelia Earhart, Jackie Cochran and the like (there were 99 of them). So we did.

We continued their mission, fun and work in the aviation industry. Painting compass roses on airstrips, creating and participating in fly-ins and air races, and sponsoring pinch hitter courses for spouses of pilots.

By now, working in the world of finance (I was a stock and commodities broker, doing retirement and estate planning as well), I really needed the perspective the flying brought! And, I was part of a metaphysical group doing my best to understand me. Hence the attraction to clearing and cleansing and filling up with joy. Life is good. Full, busy, and on track.

On My Journey!

Being in the Flow

A metaphysical gathering was introduced in Fairbanks by two lovely souls, guides on my path, when I was barely 20. My youngest brother and I attended as we were both on this spiritual, metaphysical journey that is often inspired in environments such as Alaska that are awe inspiring, sometimes serene, and reflective. Who are we? What am I doing here?

By then, a group of four folks had literally and physically shown up at the foot of my bed in the middle of the night ... turned out they were deceased, and I had been awakened by them, so I asked them to leave. It was then I tightened the filters I had developed, and decided to remind these souls that I was alive, in physical form on earth, hence their desire to get messages through me to their loved ones ... but I needed my sleep!

So they negotiated when during the day might they come? That was a tough one ... I had a very full and busy life ... yet this was part of my life too. I decided to tell them to find a way for their living loved ones to come to me, and then the communication would be easy. I wasn't ready to set up shop as a Medium, I was a stock broker for heaven's sake!

So I didn't tell any of my clients about this fabulous group of people who also channeled, saw auras, knew of books and crystals and Tarot. Though I counseled people (on the side).

I was still living as a whole person, understanding myself and life more as it went along. One pleasant Saturday, I decided to take myself to lunch. A destination was in mind, but as I drove along, I found myself desiring and heading to a different place; my favorite bakery/cafe/bookstore. It had only been a couple of days since I was there, and as curious as I found this, following my instincts has always been natural and served me best. As I pulled in to park, the inner drive to go in to the bookstore first was strong, so even though hunger was making noise, I followed that voice and entered the store. Okay, what section am I heading for? I'll just stay aware, and walk through with eyes open. Barely in, out from a book aisle pops an acquaintance ... who immediately smiles and greets me "Oh! It's you! I wondered why I had been sent here today! Let's go have lunch and chat!", she says. Okay. It turns out that she was also born as a whole, aware person, and her Grandmother had told her that one day she would be called upon to share some important knowledge and intuitive techniques (specifically, intuitive Tarot as a tool) with one important person ... that was to be me, she said. And so it was that this guide appeared for me. We had just a couple of sessions, and she thought that I was seeing and intuiting plenty, and encouraged my trust in this journey. Tarot became one of the tools I use to focus this channeled information for others.

As long as I stay in the flow, being, going, doing what feels right, life works for me. As for everyone, as long as I see that none of my thoughts, words or actions harm anyone else, I'm good! Intentions have to be set though ...

On My Journey!

Alaska ... the extremes

I have always awakened happy, especially as a small child. I loved, and love, life. It was comfortable having deceased souls and other loving entities around ... there was not an obsession with them, they were simply there, familiar to me and I didn't know life without them. Being quite human (a whole person, remember?) I enjoyed lots of friends ... and was not obsessed with them either!

Spending time alone to be quiet or to fly, or fish, or hike, or ski is solace to me. Particularly in this serene and beautiful setting of interior Alaska. And being alone is relative.

I'm quite capable of cooking and cleaning, as are my brothers and sister, but anything outdoors, particularly when the sun is out, is far more appealing to me. We are all also versed in changing a car tire, being Alaskans after all. Education, in schools and in the wild, was paramount. Anything essential to life existence doesn't have a gender. Some people are just more inclined, whether by desire or by physical or mental capability to one thing or another. And thank goodness! We find our niches, our passions and blisses, and life as a whole balances out. I had and do have passions ... flying and scuba diving, reading, hiking, camping out, fishing ... Working many more hours than sleeping or playing kept my priorities straight in that department! When time was free, I was up in the air or down at the river or gardening, hiking or taking photos of the Aurora Borealis. I cannot remember a single moment in my life that I was bored.

2a and the heat goes out in my house. When it's 40 or 50 below and colder, you tend to sleep a bit lighter, almost with one ear, one eye, and your "other" senses" open. If you sleep deeper, the disappearance of that wonderful heat will absolutely catch your attention! Either way, I awoke enough to know that I had to get out of bed and warm myself and my house. It took a few minutes to assess just how cold it had become, as I was under a pile of comforters up to my chin ... and felt the cold.

I normally arose at 5a due to the time difference between Fairbanks and New York, and the various stock and bond market openings around the world. Three hours sleep was precious, but so was not freezing to death! Literally. And if the pipes were starting to freeze, that's a whole new bag of worms, and one that needed to be prevented. My house had oil heat, and had a small wood stove on the first floor (split level house) in the rec room. I kept a cord of wood stacked outside against the house, and about half a cord inside the attached garage.

Entering the cold to participate with it when you expect it, dressed in layers of long johns and parkas, is one thing. Getting out of bed at 2a, no parka in sight, even if you're half awake and aware that cold happens, takes an entirely different state of mind and experience. It's my existence, my choice, and no one else in my house. I choose to live, and to be warm, and to prevent costly damage and time. So up I popped, quickly, and dressed warmly, quickly. First out to the garage for an armful of wood for the stove. Kindling was ready, and the fire started nicely for me (Thank Goodness!). Did I mention how small this wood stove was? For a split level house of this size, as cold as it had become, it seemed small, but was an average size stove. So I napped for 20 minutes or so at a time, needing to throw more wood on the fire for the next hours, until the repair folks were up and working to look at my furnace. Fortunately, no pipes froze this time, the furnace was fixed, and I got to work when I got to work. Warm and safe.

It was a time of working half days anyway (12 hours a day), and I had become used to the "survival" mode that simply is a way of life in Alaska. I had been truly minding my own business, sleeping even, when this happened! And I had been as prepared as an Alaskan can be. So you love it, you commiserate about it with whoever else went through it, you laugh about it, and life goes on. You're alive, after all, and feeling more alive and grateful than ever!

If it warms up enough on the weekend, at least to the low teens below zero, then cross country skiing in the pristine sparkling white snow with only the sounds of the skis on the snow, and the occasional sounds of the brave birds in the clear blue sky, beckons. There is always something to look forward to! Life is now, as you're constantly reminded, and if you stay in it and flow with it, life works. The more aware you are, the more alive you'll feel. And you'll find (and need to find) the balance ... the one short, bright, warm day called summer, and the one very long, dark, cold day called winter. Find the best in each, you'll find the best in your Self.

And then, you might decide that you care tremendously about and thrive in this environment. The beauty, the extremes, the natural and healthy food (from plants to fish to fowl to meat), the incredible people who depend on each other and find new and easier ways of life every day. Or you might decide that it would be a treat to live in an environment with many days and nights in a row; where pipes don't freeze and neither do your toes. A place where less clothing is more, and suntans last longer. As my circulation suffered (it's called Reynaud's syndrome), my digits were at risk ... it was no longer an option to have such prolonged exposure to cold. So I made a new decision, and started anew in St. Croix. Besides, when I last went there one February, I cried going back to my homeland ... just the thought of being that cold and the realization that there really was a significant difference between 85 above and 45 below; 130 degrees different! ... 7,000 miles away different. A new reality would be

80s ABOVE consistently. I could do this! So it took me five weeks, and there I was. It took a while before I quit stopping at the door in my shorts and tank top on the way outside in the morning, wondering what I was forgetting ... oh, right, boots and mittens and such! Ha! What do I need to be prepared for here, I wonder?

I meditated through this time, to keep the stress away, and to continually be one with my own spirit, my own soul. This was, without question, the correct action for me; the right path. I was joyous as I prepared, though sad to leave a lifetime of friends and family. As I drove out of the small plane parking at Fairbanks International Airport ... I had sold my airplane, and was taking one last look and feel ... there was the familiar sign on the way off the field: "Did you close your flight plan?". I finally cried. Did I need to? My greatest passion, my sanity, my joy seemed to have been partly held in this precious gift. Who was I without my plane! Well, all the rest of course, and I would fly again.

On My Journey!

St. Croix and the unexpected

St. Croix in the U. S. Virgin Islands was such a logical choice for me to move to when I could no longer tolerate the cold and darkness. Warm and a sailboat. The appeal of the warm ocean to a scuba diving, barefoot lovin', soul searching gal was simply it. When I made the decision to go, it took me five weeks to actually go. Leaving my CFP practice in my partners capable hands, selling my house (getting it started anyway), selling all my furniture and putting very little personal belongings in storage, selling my airplane and my truck, and saying "so long" to all my friends and family ... my Dad thought I had gone mad! I was, after all, established in the Fairbanks community, had more than a thousand financial clients, part of the Chamber of Commerce, etc. Even though he taught me so much about the land, the spirituality of the environment, about kindness and respect, and though he knew I had to be somewhere warmer, he said this! I believe it was his sadness speaking, and in retrospect five weeks is not much, after 33 years in a place!

So Christiansted here I am! I set up a small office for my CFP business, and soon moved aboard a 46' ketch to live on, moored out in the harbor. The friend I lived aboard with, the captain of the vessel, and I sailed the warm, calm, bluest waters of the Caribbean to the USVI and the BVI, swam with the turtles, dove the Wreck of the Rhone, and lived easy. Finally. I could be in awareness of this environment, the ever predictable warmth, lovely humidity, and pleasant breezes. The ways of the people, the creatures, all of it. Think postcard perfect. The spirits and guidance were just as present here. Truly, it's a matter of centering, clearing and paying attention. It's all there. The ocean is cleansing and safe for me; particularly scuba diving in the gentle warm water with the slow and deep resonance of your breath as focus. Nearly as blissful as flying, in a different manner.

The teak aboard shines with my constant cleaning of it; wishing for clear decks (when you live aboard, anything that can't be battened down lands on the deck, it seems), I organized and oiled. It bodes well for fitness, sun-kissed skin, a blonde braid and peaceful attitude. And there I was, minding my own business one sunny day.

Until the day a hurricane named Hugo headed our way. And that truly is a story for another day, another book. Suffice it to say that when the thing that measures wind speed blows off your boat (when you're 1/4 mile inland, 3 anchors out and tied to the mangroves with greater than 1" lines) at 237 miles per hour, all hell breaks loose! We were in a category 5 storm (unless there's another category for wind speeds in excess of 270 mph) for 12 hours; sunset to sunrise. And we never got the eye, which usually brings a moment of calm as the wind changes direction.

So the destruction was complete. The island was 98% destroyed. There was no leaf left on a tree. Not a single one. The harbors were full of oil from the destroyed vessels, right along with the dead fish and birds.

I did have an experience during that terrifying time that I will share with you, as it was life changing. As the storm approached and the ocean floor moved, the anchors strained and the lines broke! We were bouncing free in 40 to 50 foot swells, drenching with each shot, and other uncontrollable boats hitting against us. The aft mast came down, blocking that hatch ... then the fore mast came down and we were trapped inside ... moving on every axis, fore and aft, up and down, sideways too. I sat? in the galley, shaking with a terror I had never felt before ... there is absolutely nothing one can do in such an extreme act of nature.

The ocean is what I wanted; it was safety to me, and if I could only get out and into it perhaps I wouldn't die ... but I couldn't get out. It's not that I feared death; I never have. If it was time, though, get it over with! This flying through the cabin with no stability was going to break all my parts before it was done! And so I sat as best I could, actually wishing for death to come.

Suddenly, gently, I felt the strong, soft wings of powerful angels surround me, one on either side. These two angels were familiar to me from my childhood ... though it was the first I had actually seen and felt them. They took me to the place I sought. Gave me peace in the storm. Another familiar voice there told me it was time to return after my life path was once again revealed to me. Then there I sat again, after who knows how long.

Only the highlights of that path remained with me, and the bliss of our soul's home. One such highlight that was ever present, interestingly enough, was the vision of a cruise ship sailing a magnificent aquamarine sea. I held it, the vision, whatever it was to mean to me, as for now it was about survival (again), recovery, and rediscovery.

Yes, the terror remained for some time to come, as I am only human, even with this joyous experience of death. It gets in your cells, and manifests as shakes and tears, until it's cleared and cleansed completely out. Our boat ended up 1/4 mile inland in a pile of 6 other boats and a barge ... as I mentioned, there's more to the story for another time. So I shook, and I cried for years to come. When I moved, I lived in several different homes over a short period of time. I wasn't able to finish many obligations I assigned myself in an attempt to live in a "normal" way again (normal for good ole' responsible me) ... I suffered post traumatic stress syndrome; and it kept me in low self-esteem, believing we actually have no control over anything! The devastation to my heart seeing the devastation to the island, the people, the fish and birds, was long lasting. Certainly we can co-create our lives to be whatever we'd like, it just turns out better when we are free of fear and feel safe enough to have a home again. The angels and this death experience helped me survive, and over the years reminded me of the force greater than us, and of the power of this planet, and how being one with it (the force) is the alignment necessary and joyful for this life.

On My Journey! Still!

St. Croix ... why am I here again?

Days after Hugo, FEMA finally arrived. When they were finally sent, they were kept at bay on the other end of the island by armed folks who had been looting ... opportunists! And FEMA turned out to be opportunists as well. The FEMA folks drank most of the fresh water they had brought to us islanders; we were allotted barely enough to survive on though ... same goes for all the canned food; we received a can each per day of beans, only to learn later the FEMA folks ate all of the canned fruits, meats and vegetables that were supposed to be, again, for us survivors.

Ah, but I was still alive and grateful! At least I thought so until late the second day when my place in line finally made it to the FEMA makeshift desk ... and then, when asked for the registration of the boat which had been my home, I replied that it was gone ... on the bottom of the ocean somewhere most likely.

The FEMA employee simply said that if I didn't have proof of a home, then I just don't exist. Period. And that if I had received any water or food, that was a mistake.

Mind you, most all of us were homeless now. With the roofs and most walls gone from the grocery stores too, looting had occurred, so there was nowhere to get supplies of any kind. We were traumatized, lucky to be alive, thirsty, hungry, and lost souls. Grief counseling would have been nice, as would enough food and water to exist on, let alone a place to sleep. But to be told by this young man, who would not even look at me in the eyes, that I don't exist?! Wow. If he only had a clue!

Eventually, when the runway was repaired enough to be usable, and the armed men had been chased out, American Airlines came in. They offered compassion fares off the island to anywhere. Since we had stayed to rebuild as long as we could without enough to make progress, Hawaii loomed in my future ... I still needed to be warm! And I was glad to be alive.

On My Journey!

Hawaii ... On My Journey still ...

Ah! Another beautiful island after the storm. This time to live on land. What a difference to live in the 50th state rather than a US possession! The State of Hawaii brought a similar feeling of belonging as Alaska had. We had been fortunate as a family to have vacationed in Hawaii every 3 years, so even the local dialect felt natural.

The heavenly fragrance surrounds and consumes you as soon as the jet doors open, inspiring visions of flowers unique and gorgeous. All of us disembarking were from St. Croix; and to see the number of souls reaching the tarmac and kissing the ground was astounding! Such gratitude!

It felt like being right out of school again, in a world of possibilities and potential, in a magnificent land. Re-creation of one's self! With that excitement understood, where does one live? It's truly starting over. What work do I do now? Well that was made clear to me! It's by far time to share these gifts, give people guidance, pass on the messages from their dearly departed ... full time.

Well, PTSD had another idea. I wasn't confident as a person; what if that young man that said I didn't exist had a point? Of course I *knew* he was wrong, but did I? I was so shattered ... that is Post Traumatic Stress. It manifests in many ways, and is often different for each of us. So, after securing "shelter" (an apartment), I did venture out some, and attracted a few who wanted a "reading" in the park. After a short while, I gathered courage to go to a local stock brokerage, hoping the manager was still there whom I had met in years past. He was, and he worked a miracle ... bringing me into the fold. I enjoyed the industry, needed the consistent income and didn't have the confidence to do what I knew absolutely the best ... even though I've always known that doing what you love brings abundance. So I found myself back in old successful patterns of joining the Chamber of Commerce, industry groups, Kiwanis, etc. All the while also reading for people ... it's natural. And comfortable in the strong ocean breezes that grace the islands!

Friends I met were fabulous, and joined me on this journey that took me so many places and to so many homes! I loved them, the land and the ocean ... spent so much time in the active warm waters of Hawaii! It was just not in the cards to root in one place on one of those volcanic islands. For almost 7 years, I wandered that part of my journey on that part of Earth.

On My Journey With Others!

Colorado ... the happening place!

It was time to try the mainland ... I had wanted to go to Colorado since I was 3 years old ... no idea why, I just did. Well, I soon found out.

The Denver metro area is high desert with a semi-arid climate. Hot, dry summers and winters that can't seem to make up their minds! One day 60 above, the next 25 above and snowing, then melting the next day. Certainly a less extreme climate than Fairbanks, and it felt terrific to be able to drive distances again! The Rocky Mountains are actually accessible by road, which was a surprising adjustment to me. Multitudes of folks have easy access to mountain hiking, fishing and exploring these ever changing slopes that are not snow covered all year!

Perhaps I could live here and not freeze! And this move was a new opportunity for me to choose to walk the path shown to me. That meant hanging out the shingle: P.A.M. ... Psychic, Spiritual Advisor and Medium.

And so it was. Life Path Consultations is what I trademarked... a "reading" just doesn't encompass all of what I do. When I sit down with someone, in person, on the phone, or by Skype, we have a chat. Anything goes. We will connect with guidance for insight and advice regarding health, wealth, work, business, family, relationships, communications with the deceased, etc. As clients gathered, they wanted to talk metaphysics, so small groups grew; I shared, taught, guided.

Guidance brought back to me the vision from years before of a Wellness Center. So I created it, and brought in a dozen practitioners... acupuncture, intuitives, transformational therapists, hypnotherapists (me), etc. I did two live weekly radio shows.

One particularly long Friday, after a full schedule of me doing consultations, I wanted to pick up some take-out food, and go rent a movie and go home to release and get grounded. I usually balance my days with a variety of clients... this day was 100% communications with the deceased though.

All day, with more clients that I usually take. The lightness of the joyful energy of the deceased, along with the grief and the emotional release of the living passes through me, and needs to be let go. Immediately, usually.

On this particularly early evening , truly minding my own business, I was still letting go the remnants, and doing my best to bring my spirit fully back into my physical body. I drove to the local Blockbuster Video store... you remember those? As I walked in and headed to a comedy/romance section for anything light, the voice within literally boomed: "Wait! Look around! Do not leave here yet."

Okaayy... I know to listen, so I did just that, looking, wondering the store, waiting. And then I heard it: "There! Grab that one! Pay and go! Now!" Glancing at my watch, it had been 55 minutes; almost an hour. I don't know about you, but I had never spent more than 5 or 10 minutes in a video store before. So I did as I was guided to (told to, actually)... I grabbed the nearest video, and went!

In my car now, heading for takeout, when the voice, not quite so loud, had me turning into the lot of a restaurant I hadn't been to before. Wonder if they had takeout? I went in, and this nice place was packed... except for one seat at the corner of the bar that was a circle in the middle of the restaurant.

I was guided to it, so I sat and ordered twice baked potatoes or something; root vegetables are grounding for me as they help me get back into my body. Just a couple of minutes pass, and two seats next to me opened, and two new men came in and sat down, acknowledging me as they did.

Wow. The one sitting down next to me was absolutely picture perfect, gorgeous, with a very gentle soul. It's a good thing I'm not interested in getting into a relationship at the moment! This man must have 40 women knocking down his door, and I felt he was single. Not that I was checking! It just comes in, remember? I went back to my dinner, and these nice guys started a conversation with me. When the one next to me asked if that's all I was eating, I replied that yes, it was, it's my grounding food, not caring if he understood or would laugh... I was not interested! And then he asked me to explain. Holding nothing back, I did. And then he offered me his palm to look at ... more lines in one large hand than on any three people combined! ... and for the first time in my life, I saw ME in this man's palm; in his life.

And I had to tell him. It's an unwritten rule about being completely truthful about what I'm shown. The shock certainly brought me back to my senses!

Meantime, these guys shared how they had first gone to another place, went in and "it didn't feel right", so left to come to this place. Imagine that. Two I.T. guys following their instincts. And here we were. As I got up to leave, he asked for my number. He called the next night... Saturday night and I was out grocery shopping, he was home doing laundry. He said "tell me more about what you do"!! We went out the following weekend, and that was the beginning of this blessed life with my soul mate, my husband.

On My Journey With Others!

One snowy winter day

One snowy winter day a few years later, I was leaving my Wellness Center, going down the outside concrete stairwell to my car. The stairs had not been cleared of the ice and snow, but I had on my very practical flat boots! Suddenly, my feet slipped, and down I went ... all the way down the full flight of stairs, on my back. 33 years in Alaska with no falls at all, and here in Colorado I slip. Can you believe it? And I felt each fracture, each tear, each bruise as they happened. And I was in shock. Picked myself up after catching my breath, and made my way back up the stairs to call my husband. I knew I wouldn't be able to drive home, and didn't want to freeze here.

Long story short, I had eight significant injuries, including fractures, ligaments torn nearly in half, and all the discs in my neck were torn. Allopathic doctors, M.D's, told me I was permanently disabled, and there was nothing they could do for me. And as a psychic and a very sensitive intuitive, I can only effectively use natural remedies for pain and for healing. I walked when I could with two canes. After a time I worked, because I needed to; I had a business to run, needed the finances, and the pain was so extreme I would have gone batty at home. Besides, the deceased are still there and guidance doesn't quit.

As I did my best to heal myself, and after much time passed, acupuncture helped. And chiropractic. It was a slow journey for many years, to be able to walk without support and sleep through the night without pain. And nine pillows. And I persevered to heal. What a blessing to have such love for life to keep me going.

As life "normalized", I was ever more aware of the limitations of my physical body in cold weather; even cool weather... if it's less than 70 above, I feel it! Living in Colorado with a broken physical body meant adapting to a new lifestyle on this beautiful planet. What do you do if you can't ski (let alone walk well!) or fly or hike? So I adapted the best I could, and dreamed again of the subtropics.

I downsized the Wellness Center, once, and again over the next several years. Simplifying my life work and teachings. Creating the loveliest peaceful space for my clients was also lovely, and peaceful and healing for me. And continued my journey in joy ... just differently, and fully.

On My Journey With Others!

Sandals and insight ...airborne?

As I mentioned earlier, as a little girl growing up I apparently didn't like to wear shoes. Sandals and flip flops are the only way to go if you must! I had been walking pretty well, upright, on my own for a while. Moving and sitting, generally enjoying better flexibility, and able to see clients more often. Making the absolute best of it, and of this part of my journey.

Such shoes adorned my feet on this July day in Colorado. Flat, with wide silver thongs across the top. Lovely, and they kept me grounded. I walked outside in those shoes to put things in my car after a morning of clients, and closing up the car I stopped as usual with a nice deep breath, a smile and an exhale. Grateful always that it was warm! Looking up then at the unusual scalloped gray and silver clouds covering most of the otherwise beautiful blue sky, I wondered if rain will come on this warm summer day.

Hmmm, the umbrella is in the car ... I stopped again as I was walking away from it. Standing on the strip of equally gray, slightly raised sidewalk between the rows of parked vehicles, not a soul in sight, with an ominous feeling. They must all be in the lovely restaurants right there, eating, chatting and not at all concerned about a bit of weather later.

Twenty to noon, according to my watch, and oh my. What a cliff I'm on the edge of suddenly! It will break my nose when I fall that far down ... if I could only move my head a wee bit to the side! Suddenly I'm paralyzed standing here. And look at that! Visible waves of heat and energy are coming off my body, and I can't let go of the keys in my hand! That can't really be a cliff ... think, think! It's just a couple of inches to the concrete of the parking lot, isn't it? Why am I so light headed? I just need to get a grip!! But the energy surging through me is astounding and I have no control of my body, my mind, anything.

Wow! Airborne? When/how did that happen? As a private pilot for several decades, this is the first time I can recollect being airborne without an airplane! *Seems my head turned just enough though, and I've only landed on the right front side of my face ... might have cracked the eyebrow ridge or just below my eye, but my nose didn't hit and I'm thrilled about that. I do like to breathe easily! So I've landed face first down that cliff after all, or through the air where my legs still are! Where did my purse and shoes go? Interesting view upside down ... Oh well ...* a relieved exhale comes from me ... and that's all that I know.

Such incredible bliss, peace, and joy that giggles bubble up as I awaken. I see my sandals all the way over there on that strip of pavement between the rows of parked cars. Hah! I'm laying between a couple of those cars ... what a gas!

"Hello? Comes a tentative male voice; "Hello? Oh! Are you alright?" A nice young man was peering around the cars, as he saw my sandals with no one in them. *I feel such joy, and am giggling.* "Yes!" I respond as I start to sit up. He reaches me and bends to help me sit. *Ohhh, dizziness! And calmness. Glorious.*

"Lay back down while I get you a towel", this young man says. "There's a box of Kleenex in my car" I point toward it. "Your face is bleeding quite a lot. I'll go get a towel", he insists. He has looked at me as though I've become daft not to notice the amount of blood.

As I look down at my blouse, I see blood and feel its track from my eye area down my cheek and on my throat. *Where can that be coming from? It is quite a lot!* It makes me giggle more. What a beautiful day!

Two conversational, mature gentlemen approach from the direction of my head, and their thoughts are palpable. "Are you alright?" one asks me as they glare at the nice young man who has stopped to help me ... who has blood on his hand now.

"Yes!" Too enthusiastic, it must sound to them. "This nice young man" looking back at him, I ask "what is your name?" "Jason" he replies. "Jason", I giggle, "has just found me and was helping. He offered to get me a towel for the blood!"

Obviously unsettled by the uncertain looks of the two new gents, Jason exclaims

"Since you're here, I'll go back to my wife and kids. We're having lunch, and I just went out to our car to get something when I found her." And off he went as I said "Thanks!" and hope he heard.

Meanwhile, here are these very confused gentlemen, who don't know really what happened or what to do. Seems they belonged to one of the vehicles I was lying next to.

Somehow, these gents, who may or may not have introduced themselves, helped me up and into my shoes. What were they doing over there? It was where I had been standing when I felt so odd, but that is easily ten feet away from where my feet landed ... and my purse must have slid off my arm right there too.

Ah, but my keys. Right here near my hand. Made my entire palm raw meat. And my arm looks to be broken or fried, or both, but it isn't, I'm certain.

So, my watch has stopped at just 3 minutes before noon, and they tell me it's now after twelve.

So where was I for seventeen minutes? Big giggles that I cannot stop, nor do I want to, ensue.

Perhaps it's shock that takes me to the ladies room to wipe off a bit, call the friend who was going to meet me anyway, and ask her to come pick me up. The gents wanted to wait, and I was so grateful for their kindness and concern, but I don't see the point at the moment. Giggle. Nice of them to care! Truly gentlemen. I thanked them and assured them I'd be fine. They now looked at me as though I were daft. If they only knew!

When my friend arrived to pick me up and take me to the hospital, I could feel her concern and confusion. What had happened to me? I laughingly described it to her. Through her eyes, I was quite calm and extremely joyful; bleeding and blissful.

I Woke Up Giggling!

Electromagnetic shock

Electromagnetic shock that runs through the ground is also known as ground strike lightning. You don't see it coming; actually you don't see it at all. It runs through the entire body anyway. Rain isn't necessarily present, just certain atmospheric conditions.

Whether it was from the lightning itself, or being thrown through the air and deposited on my head on the concrete, either way you look at it, I was out of body for seventeen minutes.

Dead. Not a "near death experience" but an actual death experience. More accurately, a Life After Life experience. And it was glorious! Blissful! Indeed, I woke up giggling, and didn't stop giggling for many months.

When we die, transition, or go out of this Life here on Earth in any way or for any reason, it is not an experience we want to come back from. What we call death is actually another state of being for our souls that is so much more than this one ... without this dense physical body, or this brain, or these crazy emotions. It is absolute awareness, pure potential, bliss and wisdom. We *know* beyond this lifetime, and beyond this type of existence.

If you are fortunate enough to be thrown into that state of existence, and unfortunate enough (depending on how you look at it) to be thrown (maybe not literally for you) back into Life on planet Earth in a physical body, it is automatic to reevaluate whether or not you're on track for your Life Path this time around. At least for me, that's how it works.

It is easy to get caught up in everyday things, appointments, family, friends, shopping, working, eating, emoting ... and forget to focus on the big picture. What are you here for? Where's the joy? Are you enjoying this beautiful planet?

The giggles bubble up when you feel the joy. They're here to tell you what to focus on. Being dead during this lifetime (twice for me, actually), gives a person a good reminder and a positive perspective. It's a wonderful gift.

Wake Up Giggling!

Pondering this gigglefest

Pondering this gigglefest I was having all by myself, brought again the realization that experiencing joy in and of itself was good enough for this life! No rules or regulations, no shoulds or obligations, no fear. And yes, at some point does it become time to go to work or reinsert oneself back into Life? Absolutely! Passionately! And what does that look like now?

For me, I had chosen a life to be of service to others, to create a space for others of like minds and hearts, and to teach yet others who want to learn how to do so also. Sharing the bliss of Life after Life as a Medium is part of that. Mentoring those who want to practice kindness and peace, and teaching how to teach that.

Moments like this lightning strike happen, and when perceived as the blessing they are, we take the time we need to reflect and recover. Indeed I was back in a physical body, and it bled, it bruised, it swelled, and it needed time to heal. The lingering back pain from the fall years ago was gone though, due to this event. My spirit wanted time to remind me to reflect on just how I wanted to be of service, even though that clarity came while I was "dead". So many ways! I have been graced with so many gifts to share! And I live in a physical world on planet Earth where bartering is done and exchanges are made with tangible things such as money, jewelry, bread, chickens, etc. So manifesting the giving of my gifts in the circle of receiving what I need here, called for some extra meditation, visualization, thinking, feeling and acting on. Grasp it, and go! And giggle on the way.

I did take care of my physical body, and gave it time to heal. This was a quiet physical time. My short term memory suffered, and I spoke to some of the same people more than once in the same day ... thanks for your patience! My memory came fully back, as the injuries sustained from the lightning strike healed. I am grateful, as always! Each experience in life can ultimately be a blessing.

Back to my path I went when I could, doing my Life Path Consultations, for two more years.

During this time I spoke to my husband often about all the attributes of living in the warmth ... and I prepared for "when". He had lived contentedly in Colorado for fifty years. And then life manifested the right moment for both of us, He decided to go beyond what he'd always known, and travel, with me, to "warm and a beach". We decided to take an adventure, drive and move to Florida. And yes, it is the lightning strike capital of the world. And hurricanes happen here. And blizzards become Alaska, and Colorado. So I've been through my share, I think! If something more happens, well, so it does, and I will continue on. Or not! And, by the way, I am delighted to be speaking on cruise ships and loving that I'm cruising the magnificent waters of this planet again. Remember that lingering part of the vision after the hurricane? ...

Wake Up Giggling!

As an Empath

As an Empath, having this experience of being "cleared out" and re-deposited back into this body, is a true blessing. Being empathetic is one thing, though being an actual Empath is another. It is akin to being a sponge ... especially if you happen to be intuitive or a healer. I am both.

Empaths actually experience what others are experiencing as their own; particularly physically. If the experiences are not cleared from the Empath, they linger and accumulate, much as a sponge soaks up liquid and all that is in the liquid (good, bad and indifferent). If you have a kitchen sponge, for instance, and have used it to clean up spills, you will remember what it looks like after multiple uses. It must be rinsed each time, and then squeezed out so that it may dry and be ready to do its job once again. If it isn't rinsed clean and clear, after a while it becomes no longer useful and needs to be replaced, right? What we must look like from time to time!!

Having developed skills and filters which I use frequently and consistently to cleanse myself as an Empath, so as to be totally void of everything ... everyone else's emotions, diseases, negative thoughts and any of my own, it's still not quite as complete as this "washing through" of the lightning strike death experience that left me totally joyful and simply me. To pass on the clearest of information as a psychic medium, this clearing and state of being is essential. Much like a pvc pipe, a medium receives the communication input and allows it to pass through and out to the recipient, clear of their own thoughts and emotions, therefore without judgment.

So the lightning strike was indeed a gift, and I ...

Woke Up Giggling!

The doctor

The doctor who saw me when my friend took me to the hospital was either new to Colorado or new to his profession, or both. He didn't know that Colorado is rated second for lightning strikes in the U.S. So after seeing me, the blood everywhere, and hearing the moment by moment description I laughingly gave of the events, he immediately joked that I had been abducted by aliens who didn't want me so they threw me back. I thought this was hilarious! I knew he had to be joking. Then he told his staff this as though it was fact that I thought this happened.

When my husband showed up, an hour had passed ... his work was that far away. The moment my husband saw me, the doctor turned to him with a look that would freeze ice. He thought my husband did this! That wasn't so funny; interesting that this "doctor" would have such a thoughtless thought about the gentlest man around. So, this doctor did not wipe the blood from my face or my feet, nor did he ask for it to be done. He did not have an EKG or other tests done. He saw that the tops of both my feet were scraped (when my friend pointed it out) and both feet were swollen. I showed him the rawness of my right palm where the force of the lightning had exited and taken the skin off. He saw my right arm blackened, bruised and swelling. And then he gave me the only treatment he could think of, apparently; a whooping cough shot in my left arm, though he didn't tell us what it was (and it swelled too)! Ha! I tried to sit up from lying on the table, and nearly passed out ... the dizziness and giggles back again! It was a week later that we learned what this shot actually was, and what had actually happened to me, when my regular doctor returned.

This medical visit had been seemingly pointless, and My Goodness! was I extra aware of the point of things and of life in general. Upon reflection though, it was in perfect order. It was an immediate example for me of what my purpose is, a physical reminder of what I was just shown while dead. A reminder to continue to have patience, to guide and mentor others through their pain back into kindness and joy. We all have our

67

paths ... on mine I've been called a Fairy GodMentor :).

Sometimes, as evidenced by the doctor who saw me, a lack of faith in people, lack of kindness and of hearing, choosing to be in a position of service and not serving, making assumptions and acting with judgment are all potentially harmful to our fellow human beings. Assess (rather than judge) who you are, who you want to be, and who you choose to be around. Be on purpose, find faith again, practice being nonjudgmental and kind ... and discover an easier, joyful life!

Being completely joyous, it was easy to giggle as that "doctor" appeared to be disconnected from the patient and instance before him. Even when the doctor who had apparently hired him gave him a decent "dressing down" the following week, it was simply their dance ... and mine for the small part I was in. I found it fascinating that perhaps in his life, this event had to do with his position or one about to be, and whatever understanding, care, opinions he has created for himself that are important to this journey of his. His journey ... had I taken that on, I would no longer be clear or cleansed, and his position as a physician might have become too important to me. It was now time for my life again, and we had briefly touched each other's' journey ... mine to be continued on by me.

It's all small stuff, or not our stuff!

Wake Up Giggling!

Still giggling

There are those, particularly in Allopathic medicine and scientific research communities, who need to quantify, qualify, judge, and stamp with approval, what many of us already know through life experiences.

There are multitudes of others who energetically experience life, and work within energy to hear and to heal. In sharing my lightning experience, most people are simply amazed, a very few others who haven't seen ground strike lightning are certain it doesn't exist; therefore they judge that I must be nuts. There is no room for judgment in my life, so I giggle at that, and know that those few will indeed experience what they need to or not, and will continue on their path. As I go forward on mine; it doesn't matter! And those who are interested, may this event serve to enrich your own journey or to give you insight.

My husband and I had a little giggle some months after this event. As we were driving along, I noticed and mentioned the cloud formation that was similar to that day when I was the recipient of the electromagnetic charge ... it was the first I'd seen it since that moment. Thinking brilliance had struck, and not wanting him to experience the lightning energy with the keys as conduit through his arm and hand, I suggested that immediately when he parked, he should put the car keys in his pants pocket. Just as instantly, it struck us both that that was a far worse idea! The visualization was stunning and hilarious! We both giggled uncontrollably and decided to toss the keys in my purse.

So am I saintly now? Hardly (giggle)! I have been blessed once again with a broader prospective of life. It's what helps me to help others. And certainly, I'm still on my journey in this life, and quite human ... indeed an Empath who has collected again the stuff of life and the stuff of others once again. I do continue to clear it away, and serve as much as I am able to with this broad perspective. And I ...

Wake Up Giggling!

To seek the experience

You do not need to seek the experience I had in order to reflect on your own Life. Seek out that precious time every day when you can greet your soul and nurture it. You may have spent time to nurture your physical body, your mind or your emotions, though we do tend to neglect our spirit. So every day, take three deep breaths, exhaling each one. Put an enormous smile in your heart (for no specific reason), let it roam to your face, and find your calm center.

Keep that calm center, no matter what comes up throughout your day. Seek that which makes you giggle. Do what makes your heart sing, always.

After the first day or two, you may decide that your deep breathing is what keeps you living, and is bringing in joy. Breathing deeply throughout every day is what is natural

... even though you may need to relearn it. So enjoy every breath, every inhale, every exhale, and add a few more intentional ones in every day. Then perhaps every hour, then every half hour and so on until you're breathing like a champ!

You'll find health, happiness, peace and prosperity along the way this way. Why not give it a go? And rather than try, do!

Wake Up Giggling!

So what's it like?

"So what's it like?" That's the question most people ask about the "other side"; Life after Life. The next is whether or not our loved ones are there, and if so, "are they okay and what are they doing?" "Do they remember me?" "Wish they could see my kids, or my life or ...". They do!

The place we (our souls) go when we leave this lifetime is simply awesome and blissful. It's truly and instantly pain free; physically, mentally and emotionally. Visiting there is a blessing. Coming back to this Life on Earth with a renewed passion and big picture helps keep the small stuff away. Although appreciation for the small stuff is renewed also! I most always feel from departed souls who are connecting with their living loved ones is the extreme joy that is their existence. Their love for you. I also feel the grief that was present, usually from the one(s) still living.

This is another acknowledgment that your departed loved one knows what you suffered and what you feel for them now. They know you love and miss them!

"How about people who commit suicide?" That's the next question. Well, they are there in that same blissfulness also. Those living who have asked this question often express anger toward the person who took their own life. Anger is part of the grief process, so it's understandable. Please remember that where we come from, and go back to, is a place of ultimate bliss, wisdom, and a clean slate. Imagine that we are on this Earth to love one another, practice kindness, and perhaps to understand not only what unconditional love is, but what the emotion of love that humans feel, is. It's okay to be happy for your departed loved one *at the same time* you are sad for your own loss. After a time, the sadness can subside if you allow it to, and you can replace it with joy for the one departed. It is okay to move on! And the departed know you still love them! I have heard from many departed souls who took their own lives, all for different reasons. Some had negative chemical reactions in their brains due to pharmaceutical medications they were taking; the manifestations of those reactions were in the form of depression or inability to think in a rational way or feel normally. Some had severe depression due to trauma or due to physical imbalances. Some had drug overdoses. Some could not see any alternatives in their lives to turn it around. Some seemed to "stage" their death on purpose to be found by ones they chose.

Too many experiences to list, and the point is not to judge them or take it personally. It was about them and their journey, and those of us left behind may be sad or mad, but that's for us to get over. We did or didn't help them to the best of our ability. We knew it was coming or we didn't. It is as it is. It's their journey now, yours is here. Live in the present moment. Choose the best memories, learn from the rest, and be happy. They still love you, and are able to do it better now! They have a unique perspective of wisdom ... they have seen their actions, and now know what pain and other emotions were caused by them. It cannot be undone; yet it is understood and the love lacking then is in balance now. This is not to say that I'm encouraging suicide as a way to check out if you're depressed; remember that if your soul's journey is still young in this life and there is still something to learn, you may just check out only to find you have to come right back and do it all again. Get help instead if you're depressed; there are lots of loving, kind and understanding people who will assist you over this hurdle!

As souls in this human experience, we can learn from each other. Be kind, pay attention, observe, reflect on your own actions and reactions. Perhaps it's not about the drama, but rather about how we react to the drama around us. Find quiet places from time to time and reflect. Ask yourself if you are allowing yourself to wallow in sadness, anger or self-pity, or are you moving through it as quickly and as best you can with an intention of happiness and living your life to the fullest once again, and as soon as you can?

"What about my pet?" Yes, they go to the same place! And don't worry about whether or not they're being fed their special foods … they too are in spirit form, and receiving all they need! They don't truly have a physical body, they just show up that way to be recognized, much the way people do. And they're joyful! They will often show up with another loved one when you've asked for a communication … even if your departed loved one did not meet your pet in this life, they have you in common, and when you ask for that flow of love from here to there, they all show up!

"How can my loved one know how much I miss them or how much I love them?" They simply know. It is that same flow of love, highest awareness and wisdom. How would they not know? Speak it to them aloud from time to time as though they could hear you; it will do you good! You may even receive confirmation from them ...

Often in a medium connection, a living person will share with me, related to their departed loved one: "But I didn't get to say ..." or "We had a disagreement just before ..." or "How can such a good person experience ...". It's natural to be concerned about the very last words or days we had with someone (or didn't). Rest easy knowing that they know now what you want them to know! Let go. The most important thing is how we were with them most of the time. And this reminds us to randomly tell the people around us that we love them, that we like them, that we respect them. We can say those words, and/or we can show them. Being human, we can strive to be and present our very best selves to others and the world. We are here having a human experience, however, and it is through all of our relationships that we learn the most. Especially if we chose to pay attention, be kind and learn. Learn about you, about others, about Life, about Love. Then discover what you would truly do differently next time, and share that.

Those departed know and "feel" the flow of Love that you are in. Speak out loud to them, knowing they are near, they hear you, they feel you.

Wake Up Giggling!

Communicating with the deceased

One of the most important questions asked is: "Why can't I see my loved ones or talk to them if you can?"

Perhaps you can. Each of us are gifted in different ways than others. For me, the ability to communicate with those crossed over has been present my entire life. Attempting NOT to hear from or see them is the challenge. Here's an exercise for you to open to communication from your loved ones. You may already have heard from them, and brushed it off!

Sit quietly. Comfortably with no distractions. Close your eyes and put a smile in your heart as you inhale joy and peace, exhale gently all negativity (and don't dwell on what that is!). Breathe again. Be open with all your senses and imagine your loved one. Exhale again. Let the emotions wash through you and out. Notice what you feel, or smell, or see or hear. It may only be one sense. However small or large that is, really notice and acknowledge your loved one. Smile, keep your eyes closed, breathe and imagine them again. Let them come to you in the way they know you will best pay attention. Simple. Be grateful they have shown up! Let their love wash through you. Ask what you'd like, silently as they will hear you (or aloud if it's more comfortable for you). Listen with all your senses as the response may be clear or it be a metaphor rather than direct words. Sometimes the answers come later when you least expect it. Be sure to take the renewed peace you feel with you as you breathe and open your eyes.

At other times you might have had a dream, and there they were! Only it felt more real than a dream. Well, indeed, there they were. You may be too busy (mentally and physically) during the day to notice when they're around, so when you're relaxed enough they show up. Perhaps you walked into a room in your home and suddenly smelled roses or a favorite perfume/cologne of theirs ... this is another form of communication ... they are right there! You may be a person who "hears" the departed loved one. When you hear from them, don't second guess it or dismiss it; it's just as easy to imagine it's true! Of course they're communicating with you. Maybe you've felt an energy "brush" past you; this is a common caress or hug from your loved one, simply saying "I'm here!". Say hello and thanks! The more often you acknowledge these communications, the more often you'll experience them. Being calm and peaceful with an inner quiet allows you to notice the subtle energies of spirit communication.

Wake Up Giggling!

A blessing On My Journey

For me, the experience of being struck by lightning was a blessing. It was about being transported to another realm of the soul, rather than about this physical body. This was not my first death experience during this lifetime, and so being calm when returning to this body was natural ... of course I had just been in the most blissful place imaginable! No wonder my friend thought I might have gone bonkers when she saw me bleeding and battered, calm and giggling!

It's okay to be joyful no matter what's going on in your life. It's okay to experience the whole range of human emotions. It's okay to move quickly through those emotions and get back to enjoying this Life! And pay attention to what emotion and energy you bring when interacting with others. Just like putting on too much cologne or not bathing; do you want to show up that way? Do you want to show up without ridding yourself of the uglier emotions first? Do you intend to bring a smile and kindness wherever you go, or something else? However you show up to your life is by your choice; choose wisely, and show up! No decision is still a decision, remember!

Wake Up Giggling!

We all die from something!

Death is nothing to fear!   It truly is a joyful experience.   Live life now.   Do what makes your heart sings, always ... not next year, not when "xyz" gets done, not after procrastinating due to whatever you make up, now! Being happy is your birthright; be happy from the inside out.

Find your own happy ... your emotions are yours.   No one else "makes" you feel happy, sad, angry, etc. They may inspire you to a particular emotion, but those emotions are yours!   Do not give up your power to someone else by supposing that they have control of your feelings. Conversely, do not think for a moment that you have power and control over someone else's emotions!   Be happy if you will; show up happy. Hope that others will find their happy and show up with it. Be so happy that no one can shake it from you ... and if you come across someone who tries to inspire anger or sadness in you, excuse yourself and go be happy somewhere else.

We are each perfect in our own way. That said, we each find our own imperfections and attempt to perfect them. This life is a journey; we go along hopefully enjoying it the best we can. Experiencing it and making "mistakes" ... which are simply the opportunities we have created for ourselves to learn from and grow. Do it gracefully as you can, forgive yourself and notice how you will do things differently in the future. It's the School of Life! Complete with recess :).

What we don't learn during this life is okay! We get an opportunity through a life review to see the whole picture of this life time when we've crossed over, from the perspective of unconditional love and wisdom. Our soul grows.

We all die from something. A physical or mental disease, a crash, inflicted injuries, failure of the body or its parts, suicide, stress related disorders, and very rarely for an enlightened few ... we may just slip quietly and peacefully out of this body when we're done. So if you have experienced one or more of the above, and are still here, ask yourself: "Am I wanting out of this life now, or do I want healing and health and to live to my best ability?" When we stay in dis-ease (the lack of ease or balance within us), we keep that disease. Maybe that's the correct path. Or maybe it's to wake us up to pay attention to what we're doing, eating, thinking, feeling, expressing. To alert us to be on purpose; to be absolutely purposeful in this life. Maybe it's your time to go; are you going without regrets? Have you finished what you chose to finish, said what you wished to say? It was rather quick when I died from the lightning strike! And it obviously wasn't time for me to stay gone ... just a wonderful dose of the "other side" again, with a reminder that I'm on the right path and that I have much more to do here. So I choose to do it joyfully, to not sweat the small stuff, and to take care of me the best I can so that I may better spread kindness.

Imagine ultimate forgiveness in the existence where our souls come from and reside in between lifetimes. Pure bliss. No human emotions; simply joy. Imagine the balance or atonement that others souls achieve there as well; no matter what they have experienced or created in this lifetime. There is no "past" to hold on to; there is wisdom relating to love. What did you learn? What do you know to be true now? These are the questions you will have the answers to.

If you happen to be holding on to anger about something that was "done to you", perhaps it's about their life, not yours. Let go. It's for them to find the wisdom and understanding and forgiveness of self. And perhaps it's for you to forgive yourself for allowing you to be in that circumstance. Learn, forgive you, and move forward. Be as kind to others now as you wish them to be to you. If you need further understanding in this lifetime, then put yourself in their shoes for a moment. What inspired them? Remember that it takes a lot of love to put another soul through some of things we put each other through; finding the self love and expression of love to survive and then thrive is what we reach for.

Please don't waste too much of your time in the past! Experience it, learn from it, and move on ... live now! Don't let traumas and hurts of your past define you, control you, or rob you of the present. It is your choice, and yours alone to be happy now and to live now. It's a wonderful Life we live in, and you can make it absolutely fabulous with your positive thoughts and attitude.

Wake Up Giggling!

Life after Life

Death is another state of being for us as souls. We can come close to experiencing the bliss and peace of that realm sometimes through deep meditation. Happiness, contentment, romantic love are all lovely, yet do not begin to tap the extraordinary feeling of joy without stress or concern. Pure joy, bliss and unconditional love is the state of being our souls live in, in the Life after this Life. We no longer sport a body once we are deceased from this life, so that means no more pea brain and none of the human emotions we experience here, although there is a definite awareness of what those in body on Earth experience.

People ask me how I see, as a Medium, their deceased loved one, if there is no longer a physical body? The answer is that the communication from the deceased to us here in body can be in many ways that are easy and "normal" for us to notice with our six senses. So, for me, that may include the departed loved one appearing in the body they most recently sported here on Earth, or the shape of that body when they were most proud of it! In this way, I am able to describe that to the person in front of me so that there is validation that this is indeed their lost loved one. I may also hear them, sense them, smell something that is identifying of them, or simply have wisdom from them come "randomly" through. As an Empath, I also feel the incredible love they are and that they share, and all lingering grief from the one left behind.

The departed will always share feelings of their undying love, knowledge that they haven't forgotten those left behind, wisdom and information for the life of the person asking. They are often comedians and sometimes seem to play "charades" as what they communicate through me may not be literal. Also, as I speak exactly what has been shared with me by the deceased to the living, it may make no sense at all to me (and it doesn't have to), but it makes perfect sense to the recipient. Everything I receive from the departed is for someone else, not for me. It only serves if I express what I'm given, no less, no more, without judgment. We are all here on our separate journeys, each learning whatever is unique to us, on our own time frame ... it may be different for everyone, and is not to be judged, hurried, or slowed down. Sometimes we need perspective on our lives, and we want to process grief, so it's normal to turn to a departed loved one for guidance and awareness.

Your loved one always knows that you miss them!! They do know of your accomplishments, the additions to your family, etc. And they want to see you moving on, smiling, being joyful, and making the most of Your Life. It does no good for them or you to grieve long and be sad. They're incredibly blissful, and wish it for you also. You'll be together again sometime, so live in the present ... it is a present! The happier you are, the happier they are.

Joy is our natural state of being. It is what we breathe in to give life to our soul in this body, as our soul chooses to reside in this physical body in this lifetime. Fear pops up when we focus just on the physical body, the mind, and/or emotions other than joy ... especially when we don't realize that we can create whatever we want for ourselves in this life.

So Joy creates without limits! What do you imagine fear creates? More of whatever you fear, just as Joy creates whatever you enjoy. Seek joy, and create the life you truly want!

Wake Up Giggling!

To Wake Up Giggling

To Wake Up Giggling and leave behind all the stuff of yesterday, all the "stuff" of others, and imagine as I knew on that day that here is Life that I am gifted with, I decided to remember that feeling and re-experience it every day. The same body (without the judgment of its size, shape, etc.), better, though appearing temporarily worse, is what I came back to. And a moment in time that it was as it was and is what it is; beautiful, joyous, and completely unavoidable!

With that clarity, it is for me a great reminder to notice better the joy, beauty and humor that is our life, rather than the negatives. It is after all, the grace with which we respond to events in our lives that make us who we are. Gentleness and positivity, rather than difficulty, discomfort and strife are on the path to an easier, more pleasant life. Yet through the strife, we learn about life. So create what you want, enjoy it, and learn from it. Remember that like attracts like; so live in the moment, let go of fear of the unknown, and imagine the joy of what you can create (or co-create) in your life. You will always attract what you think about. If you want better, think better.

Whatever you choose to pay most attention to affects your overall outlook on life, and your consequent behavior. Please notice whether or not you are able to clear yourself enough of the negative influences of the bad behavior of the few you may be focused on to Wake Up Giggling! And if you choose to pay attention to the good deeds of others and focus on the positive influences of the many, your faith may continually be restored in humanity, and it becomes a brighter world for all of us. It already is a better world ... it's a matter of seeing it. We are a species advancing and seeing where strife needs to be corrected; rather than soaking up the negative, see the possibilities of new situations or positive outcomes, and so it will be! Pay attention, set your intent, and imagine it so!

Wake Up Giggling!

Is it possible?

Here's some fresh food for thought: Is it possible that rather than being struck by lightning, I really had been abducted by extra-terrestrials? We certainly are not the only intelligent life form that exists. And even that intelligence is questionable!

Imagine a different scenario than what you have just read (which is true for me). An existence where another life form understands and masters time and space far better than most of us do. The "beam me up Scottie" moment could have actually happened. The waves of heat I experienced around me could have been a method of transport; through time, through space, or both. If time warped, then sensing I was on a cliff was a sensation of being moved or transported. The landing on my face and not seeing my legs would have been the delivery back to Earth, and it was pretty darned close ... within 10 feet or so!

Not bad for another dimension or for extra-terrestrials of some sort.

Perhaps refocusing my memory to that of earlier awesome death experiences I've had in this life was a nice and pleasant "plant" so that I could carry on, still with the Life Path I had chosen. Perhaps there is also joy that permeates all of space (indeed!). So returning without memory of "abduction" or returning to other origins would grant me more credibility to many humans; without seeming to the general public like I really had lost it! Although it is not an unusual experience to interact with ETs or "aliens" on or around this planet, there are many who are aware of the variety of other life forms. There are numerous legends of the origin of the human species stemming from various planets and solar systems; the Star People is one such. Had my memory of being in another time/space continuum been intact, most likely I'd want to explore that more, rather than getting on with what I'm on Earth for at this time.

So, from this recent experience I don't have any lingering images of ET, spaceships, other worlds, travel through time, or anything truly exciting like that. Not to say that I haven't had communication or experiences such as some of those, as I have. Yet those are stories for another day.

In the Field of Possibilities, any reality you can imagine can exist. Anything is possible. If you can imagine it, so it is.

It is the grace with which we react to Life's curves that melds our character into aware, kind individuals, no matter what our origin.

Whatever you believe, whatever you like to think about, may become true. For me, we live in an unlimited universe full of expanding love, abundance and imagination. It is we who limit our experiences and our possibilities. It may be that the simplest of life is the most rewarding. It may be that the most expansive and experiential life is the easel for stellar soul growth. It could be that in allowing your soul to guide you through this journey is the creation of the perfect life experience for you; whether that is here on Earth or off in another dimensional experience. Whatever that becomes for you, be sure to ...

Wake Up Giggling! (At least Wake Up!)

STRUCK BY LIGHTNING AND ... WOKE UP GIGGLING!

Author Bio

Pamela Storrs is a Psychic and Spiritual Advisor and Medium, a private pilot and published author.

Alaska to St. Croix to Hawaii, and Colorado to Florida ... living life gently and to its fullest, Pam's gifts led her places where she pursues her passions of flying, scuba diving, sailing, beach-combing and enjoying friends. Formerly a financial advisor, and currently teaching meditation and guiding metaphysical gatherings, she continues her Life Path Consultations* with clients around the globe.

Her fascinating adventures while "minding her own business" during her journey through ordinary and extraordinary life in these magnificent places on Earth, inspire the grace we possess to surface, along with compassion and joy. Her writings tend to humor, and the amazing real life events she has encountered, from hurricanes to lightning strikes, wild animals to weather, may be more than you might imagine one woman could experience.

Pam continues her pursuit of a peaceful, joyful journey, without too much more of the excitement that seems to find her. We'll see! She and her husband Jim live in a quiet community in southwest Florida.

For more information about her and other books, visit her website at:

www.WokeUpGiggling.com

To contact Pam, email *Pam@WokeUpGiggling.com*

*Life Path Consultations are trademarked

www.ingramcontent.com/pod-product-compliance
Lightning Source LLC
Chambersburg PA
CBHW071820020426
42331CB00007B/1572